Gobble Wobble on the Dance Floor

Elvis Stuffingham is the laziest turkey on the farm. Why, you ask? Because he likes to eat bug candy, oink & M's, and his all-time favorite Banana, Peanut Butter, and Bacon Sandwiches.

He spends all day, every day, watching TV while he eats, and Eats, and EATS!

Bacon and Egg Oinkmint, the twin pigs on the farm, have come to visit Elvis, but they find him asleep in his chair in front of the TV. "ELVIS!" they yell. "WAKE UP! WE JUST HEARD THE FARMER TALKING ABOUT EATING THE FAT JUICY TURKEY."

Elvis nonchalantly dismisses the pigs and tells them they must be mistaken.

Bringing Elvis the proof he needs! The twins hand Elvis a picture from last year as proof of the farmer's intent. It is a picture of roasted turkey on the farmer's table.

Elvis is SHOCKED! There was no denying; he was going to be the main course this Thanksgiving. He asked Bacon and Egg, "What am I going to do? I don't want to be Thanksgiving's main course!!!!

Bacon and Egg, you have to help me! What do I need to do to avoid becoming this year's roasted turkey?

Bacon and Egg agree to help. "Come join us, and we will teach you the Turkey Flop dance."

You ain't nuttin but a noisy turkey

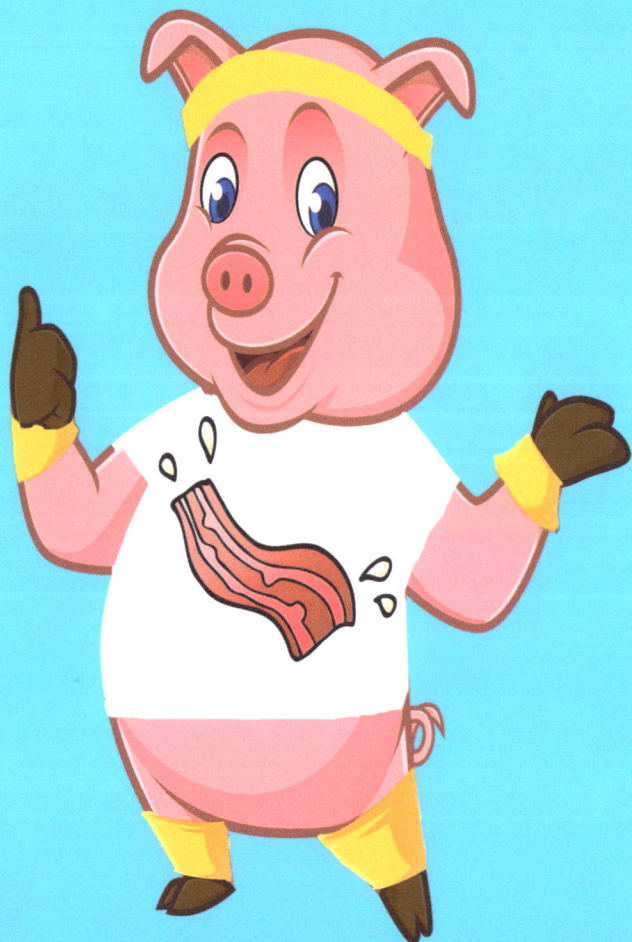

First, jump three times with us.
1...2...3...

Gobbling all the time

"Hey, wow, that was fun," Elvis said.

You ain't nothing but a butterball

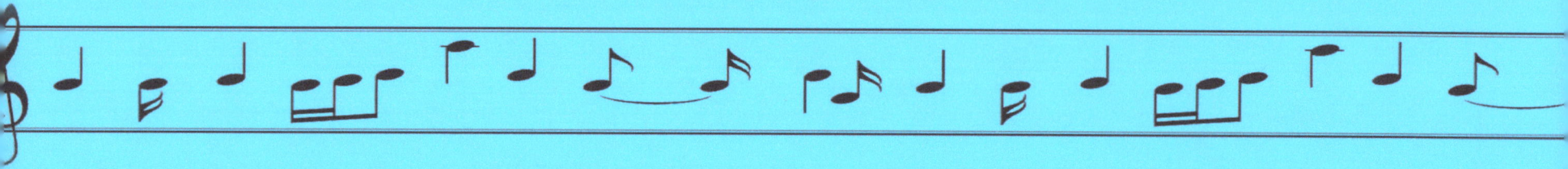

Now wave your wings and do the groove.

Snacking all the time

Come on, everyone, be like Elvis Stuffingham. You can do it too.

You snack so much but

Now it's time to shake your tail feathers;

You wont be nothing but the main dish

Moving on to Jumping Jacks.

If you are lazy all the time

Come on, we're almost there.

You are very plump and juicy

Let's jump again
three more times.

But you need to be skinny and dry

You are doing great,

Elvis!!!

You ain't nothing but a noisy turkey

Wave those wings
one more time.

Gobbling all the time

Elvis, work hard; it's not quitting time.

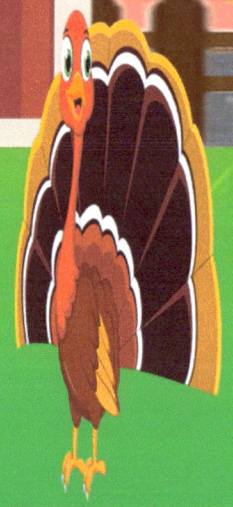

Look at me;
I am Thanksgiving-free.

The McGregor's won't be eating me!!!!!

Contributing Authors

CALEB LARCOM

ROXETTE RODRIGUEZ

Caleb Larcom: is 11 years old, he would like to be a race car mechanic. Caleb enjoys riding his bike, writing stories, playing soccer and of course video games. Caleb adores animals and has a very playful disposition.

Roxette Rodriguez: is 14 years old, and she loves music. She plays piano and wants to be a professional actress one day. She is very positive and does not believe in negativity. She is bright and loving.

SOPHIA HOWARD

SERAPHINA T. ZAMORA

Sophia Howard: is 9½ years old. When she grows up, she wants to be a cardiologist, artist, and an author. She loves to write, draw, read, swim, and play sports. Sophia is also a part of G.T (gifted& talented) at her school.

Seraphina T. Zamora: is 8 years old. She dreams of pursuing her gymnastics through college and then desires to become an engineer like her father. Her hobbies include crafting and creating new things, playing her guitar, and honing her strength and flexibility for her sport. She is kind, empathetic, and extremely energetic.

Jasmine Smith

Sydney Bucannon

Jasmine Smith: is a kind-hearted 9-year-old who loves to dance, draw, and read. She is a very active Girl Scout. Jasmine would like to be a teacher when she grows up.

Sydney Bucannon: is 8 years old and a natural leader. In 2nd grade, she read 300 plus books! She loves to dance and organize activities. When she is older, she wants to be a Veterinarian. She loves animals and people and always has a smile on her face!

Cataleya Gutierrez

Vivianna Roig

Cataleya Gutierrez: is 7 years old. She loves to cheer for the Judson Jr. Rockets Cheer team. In her downtime, she likes to sing and dance. When she grows up, she wants to be an Aquatic Veterinarian.

Vivianna Roig: is 10 years old, and she wants to be a nurse when she grows up. Vivi loves to write and read. She is quite spirited, loving, caring, and kind-hearted.

Your Children Our

Stories

CSB
INNOVATIONS

www.csbinnovations.com

www.ingramcontent.com/pod-product-compliance
Lightning Source LLC
Chambersburg PA
CBHW040404100426

42811CB00017B/1834